The
DEMENTIA
DANCE

The
DEMENTIA
DANCE

MANEUVERING THROUGH DEMENTIA WHILE
MAINTAINING YOUR SANITY

ROSEMARY BARKES

AnnotationPress

Quality Family Friendly Publishing

Annotation Press (a division of WinePress Publishing, PO Box 428, Enumclaw, WA 98022) functions only as book publisher. As such, the ultimate design, content, editorial accuracy, and views expressed or implied in this work are those of the author.

ISBN 13: 978-1-59977-049-9
ISBN 10: 1-59977-049-0
Library of Congress Catalog Card Number: 2012939423

Dedicated to the memory of my father and mother
Charles Robert Osborn and
Lois Evelyn McCracken Osborn

THE QUOTE

Although the world is full of suffering;
It is full also of overcoming it.
—Helen Keller

CONTENTS

THE PREFACE

FIVE TO EIGHT percent of all people between the ages of sixty-five and seventy-four will get dementia. Twenty percent of those between seventy-five and eighty-four will get it and 30–47 percent of those eighty-five and over will get it.

All will require a caregiver. People like you and me. We will be thrown into deep water without a life jacket. No answers will suit everyone's situation, and no job description exists.

As a caregiver I quickly learned that I did not control the circumstances surrounding dementia. The circumstances controlled me. To get ahead of it—before losing my sanity—I learned to work hand-in-hand with the disease. It's like learning a new language. Tough duty.

Emotions run rampant for both the caregiver and the loved one. Yet, the pain and heartache can be minimized if the caregiver works *with* dementia instead of against it on a day-to-day, sometimes moment-to-moment basis.

THE DEMENTIA DANCE

That's what I learned while caring for my eighty-five-year-old mother and what I believe might help others in the same boat. Even then it will be a rough ride. So fasten your seat belts and hang on.

THE INTRODUCTION

WHAT DO YOU *do* when a loved one asks, "Who died," when it was her husband of seventy years who had died just the day before? What do you *say* to your loved one when she blurts, "Don't throw that button away. It belongs to Aunt Carrie. She'll be back for it later today," when, in fact, Aunt Carrie died forty years ago?

I stood in shock is what I did, and what I said was nothing. I was too stunned to move. Thoughts like "Oh, God" or "This can't be happening" raced through my mind like a runaway train. My stomach did flip-flops.

From that moment on, what to do and what to say became a full-time challenge. Unforeseen obstacles and daily surprises ran hand in hand.

Realizing the situation would never return to "normal," I dealt with those unforeseen obstacles as best I could. I was not prepared for the mental, emotional, physical and spiritual spin-offs. Coping became the order of the day.

I sought outside help. Family members, friends, doctors, nurses, social workers and ministers were all there for the asking.

Seminars can help. I attended a few and learned about the latest medicines available to dementia patients. I learned which meds don't mix. I also learned about the link between age and dementia.

Ultimately what I learned—from observation and experience—was that dealing with dementia was much like "dancing with dementia." A partnership if you will, with your partner *always* in the lead.

The dance can be slow and smooth, even with a certain ease and flow. But more often than not it is turbulent, like a punk-rock gathering.

The latter was especially evident during the early stages of Mom's dementia when we had to move her from her hometown of eighty-five years to where I lived fifty miles away.

The former, with its ease and flow, became a mere shuffle throughout the last stage. And, finally, the music stopped altogether.

CHAPTER 1

THE FIRST CLUE

MY FIRST STEP in "dancing with dementia" came without warning, at a time when I was least prepared for it. Three days after my ninety-one-year-old father's unexpected and sudden death from a brief bout with pneumonia.

The immediate family had gathered at the house where Mom and Dad had spent their last forty years, keeping busy until the bewitching hour arrived. We were to travel as a caravan to the funeral home for the viewing. Small talk and nervous laughter prevailed, along with a few lame jokes to lighten the atmosphere. Mostly, however, there was sadness and silence.

Out of that silence—suddenly—Mom asked, "Who died?" Her eyes were shining and she had a radiant smile on her face.

My siblings and I looked at each other and froze. Surely what we thought we heard was not what Mom had said.

We stared at her. There she sat, dressed in her Sunday best: a gray striped suit and long-sleeved red blouse peeking out from under the neck and sleeves of her jacket. Unsure of what to say, I leaned into her and whispered, "Mom, *Dad* died."

"Oh," she said casually, fiddling with her white, lacy handkerchief, as if it were just another day. I was numb, still trying to process what had just happened while retaining my composure. What on earth was going on?

Dad had told us kids during our visits the last couple of years that Mom was failing, and how much it distressed him. He would sit in his rocker; chin quivering, tears rolling down his cheeks, muttering, "It hurts to see her like this."

We underplayed his emotions because he was, by nature, given to emotional outbursts. He cried more often as he aged, especially after our brother Ron was killed in an automobile accident in 2003. We thought he was exaggerating about Mom because, try as we may, we couldn't spot any changes in her.

I am ashamed to say that not one of us pushed for details. The few times we did, he would simply say, "She's just … different," and let it go at that.

That particular response was not unusual in our family. The saying was, "What you don't know won't hurt you." More than once I heard Mom say that if she had cancer, she didn't want to know about it. When Dad would come home from a doctor's visit and we questioned him about details, he would counter with, "I don't know. I didn't ask."

Plus, when they were together, as they always were, Dad, who was the more outgoing of the two, often answered for her and always had. It was a dance *they* had done for years: him in the spotlight; her, second fiddle.

Mom still baked our favorite desserts when we visited, hugged us and seemed happy. Plus, she looked the same, dressed in her jeans or slacks and shirts or sweaters, shoes always tied. If her hair wasn't curled, we figured it was time for a perm.

It wasn't until after Dad died and I picked up his medical records, plus hers, from the physician's office that I saw she had been diagnosed with "onset of dementia" (short-term memory loss) two years earlier. I could hardly get my breath after reading that and realizing how insensitive we had all been to Dad's plea for help. It was a sin of omission we had to live with.

CHAPTER 2

THE VIEWING

IF MOM WAS "losing" it here at home, what was ahead for the viewing? Would she react as we always suspected she would—overcome with tears or wails of sorrow—or would something unexpected happen? I cringed at the thought.

At the funeral home I gently took her by the elbow to see Dad in his casket. I was shaking each step of the way from seeing my dad for the last time and from fear of what Mom would do or say. My feet felt like lead.

Much to my surprise, she simply said, "He has on his favorite tie. Doesn't he look nice?" I waited for her to say something else, but that didn't happen. No emotion. No hint of loss. It was as if she were at a neighbor's funeral instead of her husband's of seventy years.

I, however, made up for her nonchalance by softly crying. In my mind, "The Lost Chord" was playing ever so faintly. More than once when Dad and I listened to it together, he would say, "I want that played at my funeral."

"Me, too, Dad," I would echo. Of course, at that time, the idea of death for either of us was but a vague notion.

On one of those occasions, he gave me hand-written, detailed directions on how he wanted his funeral to be conducted. He wanted to be buried in his grey trousers, red-and-white-striped shirt, red-and-gray-striped tie, and wine jacket.

Mom was right: he did look nice. I could hear him saying, "Good job, Rosemary. I knew I could depend on you. Take good care of Mom."

While I had successfully done everything he requested for the funeral, would I be able to successfully carry out his other request?

Knowing I had guests to meet and greet, I dismissed the thought and silently mimicked the words from Scarlett O'Hara in the movie, *Gone with the Wind*, "Fiddle dee dee, I'll worry about that tomorrow."

CHAPTER 3

THE QUERIES

AND WORRY I did. About what to do, how to do it, and who would do it. The *when* was obvious. *Now!*

The three of us siblings wanted to be there for Mom, but being there for her did not mean we could be there *with* her. I lived fifty miles away; my sister, 150; my brother, out of state. All of us were married.

Brother Dan was in the process of rebuilding his life with a new wife and a new job. He had recently moved to Tennessee. With these challenges facing him, the best he could do would be to keep in touch with Mom through the telephone and cards.

Sister Karen lived two hours south of me. She and her husband, Jerry, babysat full time with their two young granddaughters. Chasing down an active toddler and cuddling a newborn left scant time or energy for extra duties.

I was it. I was retired and blessed with a loving husband who would support me in any decision I made about caring for Mom. Even though I was involved in several community groups and volunteered at an assisted-living facility, it made sense that I would be the main caregiver. I could juggle other commitments.

Mom could make her new home at the assisted-living facility where I volunteered, and I would be available around the clock. The fact that I was executor of the estate and had power of attorney cemented the decision.

After observing Mom's off-the-wall behavior before, during, and after the viewing, Karen and I decided we would each spend two weeks with her to assess the situation: gather information from her doctor, nurses we knew, the minister, and those we knew who had once been where we were. We would then compare notes.

Karen took the first watch. She and her husband, Jerry, did research on the value of the two cars that now belonged to Mom and came up with a plan for their disposition—when the time was right, because Mom still wanted to drive.

Karen spent considerable time sorting through Mom's medicines and talking with the pharmacists about the need for each and every one. She took Mom out for lunch and other side trips, keenly observing ways Mom had changed.

When it was my watch, I headed for the doctor Mom and Dad had been going to for years. I was hoping for some solid advice. Instead, he handed me the medical records of both Mom and Dad. "Your mom has short-term memory loss and has had it for two years now," he said.

I stared in disbelief. Two years? Dad had been living with this for two years? He had never mentioned the word dementia to any of us.

The doctor brought me out of my stupor by saying, "I don't want the responsibility of deciding whether your mom should stay at home or be taken to an assisted-living facility, but I will tell you that she has balance issues. Going up and down steps could be dangerous." End of story.

I hurried home and counted the steps from the first floor to the basement. Twelve. Mom often did the laundry or fussed around with her crafts down there. If she lived alone, that would be a constant worry for us.

From nurses and friends, the consensus was that having in-home care was not a good thing. Too many unknowns.

The minister that Mom and Dad loved was quick to respond. "For quality of life," he said, "I recommend assisted living." He proceeded to tell us that living at home usually resulted in quick deterioration of both mind and body. He used church member Dorothy as an example.

Dorothy stayed in her home after her husband died, but stopped going to church, stopped going to the grocery store, and stopped seeing friends. When the minister visited, he found that her hair had become matted, she wore no makeup, always had on the same grimy robe, and was not brushing her teeth. His visits were typically in the middle of the day, yet the drapes were consistently closed.

He reported her condition to her daughters, who lived out of town. They quickly moved their mom to an assisted-living facility. There she flourished.

As feisty as Mom was, would she agree to give up her house of thirty years, her beloved town, her church and her friends?

It would probably take an act of God for that to happen.

THE AGREEMENT

BECAUSE TIME WAS of the essence, we couldn't wait for an Act of God. Karen and I quickly agreed that Mom could not stay alone. Not only was her short-term memory an issue, but the house was also starting to look grungy.

The hood over the stove was grimy with grease and dirt. A deep crevice showed gunk when I ran my finger over it. That hood probably hadn't been wiped off for two or three years ... or more.

God love Dad. I'm sure the thought of swiping across the hood of the stove had never entered his mind. It was so-o-o-o far down on his list of priorities.

He had been consumed with the grocery shopping, the cooking, the running of errands, the dispensing of Mom's pills and eye drops and paying the bills. God love 'im.

Stacks of envelopes and magazines were piled on the two side tables in the family room. Some were propped up against the front of the sofa and the ottoman. All askew.

One day I watched Mom hustle to greet the mailman and retrieve the daily allotment. She plopped down on the sofa afterwards and opened the envelopes in front of me.

After slicing through them, she glanced at each one casually and threw them onto the nearest pile of mail. I spied a few bills among the junk mail and thought, "Yikes. This is trouble right here in River City." I made a mental note to sift through her mail at the end of each day after she had gone to bed. That way I could weed out the priorities and follow through on them.

The cupboard doors were smeared with murky fingerprints, especially around the handles. The windows were streaked inside and out from years of neglect, and the carpeting was soiled from the wear and tear of thirty-plus years. Dirt and dust had accumulated along the edges, making it shades darker than normal.

The drapes in the living room and dining room were faded, and the bedroom curtains were yellow from age and neglect. Funny how it never bothered me before Dad died and I found out Mom had dementia.

Mom wasn't making any effort to cook or bake, activities that had always been favorites of hers. She claimed not to be hungry.

One day I let the entire day pass without suggesting we eat, just to see if she would take the initiative to fix something for us.

Okay, okay, I lied. Before bedtime, I fixed a bowl of raisin bran and sliced up a banana for the two of us. I couldn't help it.

Mom also did not make an effort to flush the toilet anymore. When I reminded her of it, she didn't seem the least bit concerned or embarrassed. The Mom I once knew would have been horrified.

She had trouble deciding what to wear each day. Her standing at the door of the closet, shoving the blouses back and forth—over and over—in search of the right one, was beginning to drive me nuts.

I was getting really impatient. "This looks like the one for you to wear today, Mom," I would announce, then try not to yank that piece right off that hanger in anger. With a smile on her face, she readily agreed to wear what I suggested. She never argued about my choice.

This was not the efficient, organized, no-nonsense woman my brother, sister, and I had known all of our lives. This was someone else. And because she was someone else, we would have to become someone else as well.

CHAPTER 5

THE CONFRONTATION

OUR HUSBANDS AGREED that there was no way Mom could live in that house alone. They also agreed to back us up in our confrontation with her.

We picked a specific day and asked Mom to join us in the living room. She walked in with a smile on her face and sat in Dad's rocker. Karen and I sat on the sofa surrounded by our spouses.

In our family, the man was boss and made the final decisions, so Karen and I deferred to our husbands to break the news to Mom that it was time for her to think about moving.

Jerry spoke first. "You know, Lois, you can't live alone in this house anymore. The steps are too much for you and it's not safe for you to live alone."

Before he could utter another word, Mom blurted, "Sure I can. There are many women who live alone in this town. Look at Thelma down the street. She lives alone."

We were quick to remind her that Thelma's grandson lived with her and others had relatives in town who could look in on them every now and then.

My husband John added, "If you fell, Lois, no one would be here to help you."

"You can go if you want to, but I'm staying here," she said stubbornly.

I had to steel myself from bolting from the room. Of course she didn't want to leave. Yet, there we were trying to get her to see things our way—rationally—as if her feelings didn't matter. I looked at Karen and Jerry, then John. They were collectively staring at the floor. Where was that Act of God we so desperately needed?

CHAPTER 6

THE LIE

MOM WOULD NOT budge. Her friends, her church, her neighbors were as much a part of her as her DNA.

My heart ached for this woman who gave birth to me at age seventeen on my grandparent's farm. She often told me how she was placed on a blanket made of newspapers when my birth was imminent. My father and both paternal grandparents were standing by for support. No doctor was on hand.

When I arrived—and she never mentioned the pain of childbirth—my grandmother reached for me and hollered, "There she is! She's beautiful! Give her to me!" That's my story, and I'm stickin' to it.

Mom stood straight up from the rocker, pursed her lips and squinted, "You people can move if you want to, but I'm staying here." She spun around and left the room. So much for the rational approach.

I headed to our attorney's office, desperate for suggestions. He had one, and one only.

You'll just have to lie.

THE DECEPTION

LIE? TO MY own mom? The same woman who would not lie for me when I was a teenager and didn't want to take a phone call from my boyfriend? I had asked her to lie for me by telling him I was not in. I fixed it eventually so she wouldn't have to lie. From that point on, when a boy called and I didn't want to talk, I would quickly open the back door and step outside until she had done the dastardly deed. That way she didn't have to lie.

I cringed as the attorney spoke. "I had to lie to my mom. It's not easy, but it's the only way," he said. I knew that his mom was in an Alzheimer's facility an hour away and had been for several years. I figured it was easy for him to be rational about it.

He gave me specific directions to follow. I hurried home and told Mom there were papers for her to sign that day, and she believed me. There had been a plethora of papers to sign early on as we proceeded with the managing of the estate, so it appeared to be a routine errand.

The anxiety and frustration were almost unbearable as I tried to get Mom moving. I was sick at heart deceiving her and dreading what the future held for her and us. Yet, I needed to get on with it. I wanted off the rollercoaster.

I could not rush Mom as she dressed. She stood there, staring into the closet where her colorful blouses and polyester pants hung neatly in a row. As I stared with her, I was mentally selecting which ones to surreptitiously stuff into an overnight bag for the assisted-living complex. It had to be a small bag which could be stashed in the back of the van where she wouldn't notice it.

She stewed over which handkerchief to tuck into her pants' pocket. Over and over she looked at the pile of them, remarking about the colorful embroidery on each.

When we finally got to the kitchen, she stewed over her money. She opened her money box and counted her dollar bills over and over, deciding how many to take. I wanted to scream.

Instead, I grabbed a Bob Evans carry-out paper bag and headed to the bathroom for her toiletries, then to the bedroom for a couple of outfits to last her until we could return for more.

By the time Mom and John got to the car, I had already stashed the Bob Evans carry-out bag into the back of it.

Never in my life had I felt so rotten … ashamed … guilty. How could I live with myself?

CHAPTER 8

THE OPTION

MY SAVING GRACE was that Mom was going to a place I *knew* she would like. I had been volunteering there, just minutes from my home, for nearly four years. It was an outreach program the Methodist Church provided for members who could no longer attend regular services. There were two couples I visited on a monthly basis.

Colony Court was charming, clean and well furnished, had a friendly atmosphere and a myriad of activities for its residents to enjoy. Exceptional care was the norm.

While volunteering one day, I witnessed executive director Dee perform her magic. Frances, a dementia resident who seldom talked—mostly sat and stared— was sitting in a chair blocking the doorway of the director's room. Apparently someone had inadvertently moved it there.

Director Dee squeezed by the chair from her office and grinned at Frances. Tony Bennett was crooning "I Left My Heart in San Francisco" on the boom box. She took hold of Frances' hands and said, "Let's dance, Frances. Tony Bennett is singing." Frances stared, but reluctantly stood up. Dee placed their arms in the proper position for dancing. "Now Frances, move your right foot toward me," she said, pressing her own foot against Frances' right one.

Again, Frances simply stared. The handful of us who were sitting and watching in the lobby, also stared. Frances finally moved her foot.

Her eyes drifted toward Dee. "Now, Frances, move the left foot," she said. Once again, slowly—very slowly—Frances did as she was told. This dance continued until the two of them were clear of the chair. "See there, Frances. You can still dance!" Dee helped Frances sit down on the sofa, then lugged the chair out of harm's way and headed for her office.

The rest of us clapped and shouted, "Way to go, Frances. Way to go, Dee." Frances sat there stone-faced, as usual; Director Dee returned and took a bow.

I knew right then and there that if I ever needed to be in an assisted-living facility, Colony Court would be it. Never in my wildest dreams, however, did I think my mom would be a resident.

Mom liked to ride in the car and look at the sights, so I had taken advantage of it and driven the fifty miles to Colony Court for lunch one day during my two week "watch." At that time, I suggested she might like to stay. "Oh no," she said, "This is nice, but I wouldn't want to live here."

I knew Mom was a strong-willed person. She would fight like a cat if cornered. Was I strong-willed enough to fight back?

CHAPTER 9

THE MEMORIES

A PALE BLUE sky with white puffy clouds was overhead when John, Mom, and I headed out of town. Mom was in the passenger seat marveling at them. She had a sing-song voice when she spoke of the clouds, the sprawling farms, herds of cattle, silos, and the fairgrounds where her grandfather had once been a driver for horse-drawn sulkies. We were leaving behind the town where she had lived her entire life and where my siblings and I grew up and graduated from high school.

Mt. Gilead. It was actually a village, the county seat, where my dad had been employed for forty years at the HPM company, which made plastics, among other things, and my mom worked part-time at Kresge's ten-cent store years before. My dad and siblings worked at the Union Department Store which no longer existed; I, at the local newspaper, the *Register*, carrying papers once a week to Whiston's Drug Store. My grandmother,

Ruth Osborn, was editor of the society page and handed me the job for fifty cents per trip. I saved every penny of it until I could afford a small white Arvin radio.

The main streets were lined with staid maple trees standing like toy soldiers, protecting the local residents who walked or drove under them.

A sizable monument—a victory shaft—graced the center of town. My dad was a lad of five when it was erected in 1919. "The landmark is a Victory Shaft," he would boast, "A gift from France for our county selling the most war bonds."

Surrounding the monument when I was growing up, were two parks. One was on the southeast corner and one on the southwest corner. A candy-apple man sold his wares on the southeast corner in the summers. Community events were held on the southwest corner. There were restaurants on both the northwest corner and the northeast corner.

One restaurant—The Inn—was replaced years ago by a bank. Before Interstate 71 was built, people drove for miles to eat there. It was a well-known spot for travelers because it rested between Cincinnati and Cleveland.

It was there that my friends and I would sometimes spot Bob Hope, if we were lucky. He would be with his brother, Fred, who lived near Mt. Gilead.

If you are not from a small town, you need to know there was scant little to do on *any* given Saturday night, especially in the 1950s. Even the *possibility* of seeing Bob Hope in person was as good as it got.

Our ritual was to plop down in a large booth at the hangout across the street from The Inn, watch from the large front window and wait. Hoping to catch a glimpse of the famous star.

When he did show, he busied himself shaking hands with those within his reach, smiling that big smile of his and chatting as he entered the restaurant. It wasn't much, but it was plenty good for those of us who were star struck.

Legend has it that the owner's (Mrs. Kimmey's) lemon meringue pie was what drew him and his brother there. Thanks for the pies, Mrs. Kimmey, and thanks for the memories Mr. Hope.

CHAPTER 10

THE TRANSITION

WHEN WE PULLED into the parking lot of Colony Court, Mom blurted, "What are we doing here?"

I took a deep breath. "We're having lunch here, Mom. We've been here before," I replied.

It was a blessing that I had been volunteering there. I knew the first names of all forty-nine residents and the names of the staff members. The director had quickly found a room for Mom when she had needed it.

We were met at the front door by Executive Director Dee, who promptly ushered us to the dining room. "Welcome, Lois, let me take you to your table, reserved for you and your family," she smiled.

Curious looks followed us. It reminded me of a classroom setting when a new kid walks into the room of a school for the first time.

Some folks stopped eating long enough to take in the new faces and whisper to their neighbors while staring at us. Some continued to eat in silence.

Several hands reached out to me along the way, acknowledging my presence. Mom was quick to react, "Do you work here? Everyone seems to know you."

We ate our lunch in the sunlit room and made small talk. "Isn't this food good, Mom? It's your favorite, candied carrots," I said. She nodded and remarked about how nice the place was.

When I leaned in to ask if she would like to live here, she replied, "Oh no. It's a charming place—nice and clean—but I'm going to stay in my house."

"Heaven help me," I murmured to myself, "What am I going to do now?" Those mashed potatoes that earlier had gone down easily suddenly stuck in my throat.

CHAPTER 11

THE AGONY

DIRECTOR DEE STEPPED in by asking Mom if she would like to see her room. I nearly fainted waiting for a reply. I felt suspended in air like a helium balloon until Mom finally spoke, "Well, I guess I can look at it, but I won't be staying."

The long trek down the hallway to room 63 seemed endless, as if we were walking in slow motion. The fully furnished room with lace curtains and newly laid dark-green carpeting welcomed us. The smell of "new" permeated the room. Sun shone brightly through the curtains. It felt as if Mom belonged there. It felt like home.

"Isn't this a nice room, Lois?" Dee asked.

"Yes it is," said Mom, "But I can't stay. I would need to discuss this with my family."

I began to shake from anxiety. "Mom, you have already discussed it with us. You just forgot," I said.

She must have felt like a cornered animal because her eyes darted back and forth between Dee and me, fear racing through them. I had to look away.

"I want to go home," she pleaded as she wrung her hands and turned toward me. I felt as if I were drowning, a replay of earlier times when I nearly did. Before I could swim, I accidentally jumped into the deep end of the pool and rolled round and round, flailing beneath the cold surface; helpless, desperate. Eventually, my uncle saved me. Who was going to save me today?

Dee did. "Lois, let's just give it a try, okay? You don't have to stay if you don't like it. Just give it a try," she said. Silence hung heavily in the air as the sun's rays continued to splash across the room and onto the new carpet.

Dee broke the agonizing silence by repeating, "Lois, just give it a try. If you don't like it, we'll figure something else out."

"Like what?" Mom blurted immediately. Dee was silent.

By now John was yanking at my sleeve. "Let's go," he whispered, "It's not going to get any easier." He knew from experience with his father who had suffered from Alzheimer's years before.

I quickly moved to Mom's side and hugged her, saying, "I'll be back to have dinner with you tonight." I did not wait for a response. I grabbed John's arm and bolted.

CHAPTER 12

THE LOVE

COLONY COURT, WITH its light gray siding, neat white trim, boxwood bushes, and long front porch awaited me as I drove up at the dinner hour.

Never did I appreciate Mom more than that night when I stood at the front door of Colony Court. There she was, sitting in the back of the dining room at a small table with three tablemates. They were busy eating, but not talking.

Servers were scurrying around, smiling and chatting with residents as they placed food from their carts in front of each one. Mom was smiling, too. Thank God.

My heart swelled with pride. There she was, cutting her meat, sipping her coffee. Not a hint of being rudely uprooted. No sign of remorse from the death of her husband, his cemetery plot still covered with mud from his burial a month earlier.

Because of my recent emotional state regarding Mom's dementia, I had temporarily forgotten how pretty she was. Her curly white hair was combed neatly, and she had good color in her cheeks. The pink cardigan my sister gave her made her look soft and feminine.

"Oh Mom," I sobbed leaning against the door frame, "You didn't ask for this. It's simply a nasty trick of fate. What does the future hold for all of us?"

I reached down into my coat pocket for a tissue and wiped my eyes and nose as best I could. No doubt my eyes were red, but who would notice? Or care? The important thing was I was there as a familiar face amidst the sea of strangers. Plus, I promised her I would be there for dinner and wanted to keep that promise.

Undaunted, I grabbed the doorknob and went inside thinking, *Maybe Karen and I made the right decision to bring Mom to Colony where she will at the very least be safe and surrounded by other people.* I hurried to be near her.

As I crossed over to the table, I mumbled to myself, "Thank you, Mom, for not staying in your room sulking, for not sitting on the edge of your bed staring out the window, and for not cutting yourself off from the other residents."

She was surprised to see me as I slid in beside her, dragging a chair from a nearby table. A sweet young staff member brought me a cup of coffee and a piece of chocolate cake.

I did most of the talking, getting the names of the tablemates plus a little of their personal history. I shared a few things about Mom to them and tried to engage her in the conversation. She, on the other hand, seemed content in simply eating her meal.

My thought was that after years of serving others it was a pleasure for her to be waited on by someone else.

As we finished up dessert, I took Mom's hand, kissed her on the forehead and told her I would be back the next day. On the way to the car I felt like jumping up with a heel click. Instead, I gave myself a "high five." This was a good start. Would it last?

CHAPTER 13

THE CALLS

AS SUSPECTED, I had patted myself on the back too soon. While Mom's days were filled with crafts, Bible study, exercise class, and pet therapy, her nights were not!

Between 7:00 P.M. and 7:30 P.M., the phone calls came. The pleas were always the same, "Rosemary, I want to go home. Why did you put me here?" The voice was barely audible, more of a desperate whine.

Guilt gripped me before, during, and after each call, leaving me with feelings of helplessness and sorrow for her inability to control her own life. I ached for her. I wondered how I would respond if my own daughter had uprooted me and moved me into an unfamiliar place. "Don't go there," I reminded myself.

I tried to reassure her. "I know you want to go home, Mom," I replied, "But the doctor said you have balance problems, and Daddy would want you to be at Colony where it is safe."

"No, he wouldn't," she would blurt, then sob.

I was consumed with guilt and dread, night after night, until my husband finally stepped in with, "I can't stand to see you like this. You're making yourself sick. You did the right thing. We're going to get caller ID."

We learned from my sister's calls that if *we* didn't answer Mom's calls, she would be next in line.

I told her the situation. While I was annoyed with the calls, I was relieved that Mom had the presence of mind to call Karen. At least she would have an outlet for her frustrations.

It was during this conversation with Karen that I asked for her indulgence in answering Mom's nightly phone calls. I was busy during the day getting the names of new doctors, arranging Mom's room, buying odds and ends for her, eating lunch with her, etc., and at the end of the day I was exhausted.

No doubt my baby sister could feel my pain because she agreed to field all future calls from Mom whenever she could. My husband and I, for now at least, had some nights to ourselves without interruption.

I shared with my sister an approach I had learned in college called "broken record," which was a consistent response to unsolicited pleas from others. It means giving the same message over and over to eliminate distractions from the main point.

Karen and I hammered out a response that we could both use. "Yes, Mom, we know you want to go home. Just give it a try; it's a nice place." That approach worked for us, but nothing could diminish the anguish we felt when we heard her desperate pleas.

Mom called one of us every night for exactly six weeks. After that, the phone calls stopped. Abruptly.

During those six weeks, even though confusion and anxiety reigned for both Karen and me, we held firm because we knew it was the right place for Mom to live out the rest of her days. It was one of the most emotionally wrenching decisions we had ever made.

CHAPTER 14

THE COSTS

MAKE NO MISTAKE about it. It costs a pretty penny to live in an assisted-living facility. At this writing it is at least $100 a day, more if your loved one requires a higher level of care than the norm.

Yet, if you can afford it, the comfort of knowing that a loved one gets three meals a day, available nursing care, companionship, and entertainment—and has at their fingertips a beauty shop and visiting doctor—makes the cost worth it.

My siblings and I were blessed. By living simply and being resourceful, our parents had squirreled away enough to pay for assisted living for five years, with the help of Mom's social security checks.

Some expenses can be controlled by the caregiver. There is no need for a lot of clothes. Life in an assisted-living facility is fairly simple, and there are no "Joneses" to keep up with.

When I once visited a resident at a nearby Alzheimer facility, I witnessed her family carrying in armloads of new clothes for her, all the while yakking over colors of the outfits and costs of them. These comments were made within range of their mother's hearing even though she was lying on her bed facing the wall and playing with an outlet. It made me sad because I learned long ago that the hearing is the last to go.

Mom had plenty of clothes when she went to Colony. The only things Karen and I bought her were make-up and an outfit for her birthday each year she was there. A little something for Christmas.

Okay, I lied. My sister loves to give presents and, looking sheepishly, would often slip in a sweater or pair of jeans for Mom. "I can't help it," she would say.

Residents' rooms were furnished at Colony, unless otherwise specified. Ironically, Colony's furniture was nicer than Mom had at home, and she was delighted with it. She and Dad hadn't bought furniture for over forty years, which turned out to be a good thing. The money saved on new furniture helped pay the bills now.

A phone may or may not be vital to your loved one. We considered a phone a necessity for Mom's independence as a connection to the outside world. It worked for a few months, but when she began to struggle with which end to put to her ear and which to talk into, and how to dial, we made the decision to cancel the service. She never asked about it.

Is TV a must? For those residents who enjoy it, yes. But for Mom, no. She would rather sit in the lobby and read or visit with the folks.

Still, we decided to bring her TV from home, put it in her room, and get cable for her. Time would tell whether she used it or not. She never even turned it on, so after three months we cancelled the cable service. Again, she never asked about it.

Thrift stores are a boon. When Mom was in the last stages of dementia at an extended care facility and confined to her bed, an aide suggested I go to a thrift store and buy housecoats with snaps on the front of them so they could put them on her backwards, leaving the back open. That would help eliminate the excruciating pain Mom endured whenever she was moved or touched.

Eating at the assisted-living facility was a lot cheaper than going out. Each meal at Colony was a whopping $5. Lunch and dinner included a salad, entrée, vegetable, roll and butter, beverage of one's choice and dessert. Most of all, it was a simple way to pass the time with our loved one.

CHAPTER 15

THE ROOM

ANOTHER WAY TO pass the time is by spending time with loved ones in their rooms. Include them in decisions concerning where the furniture and accessories belong.

Even though Mom couldn't remember her room number or how to get there, she was overjoyed when she finally did. When family members weren't there to help, staff members were.

"Is this my room?" Mom would ask over and over while staring at the brass plate, which read: *Lois Evelyn Osborn, Room 63.* I eventually hung a collage of family pictures on the wall beside her door for easier reference. Instead of looking at the brass plate, she would glance at the collage and say, "There's Poppy. I miss him."

Mom loved the cheerfulness of room 63. Light and airy from the large single window with sheers to let in the sunshine. And the carpeting was new and had that fresh, newly laid smell to it. The director had asked Mom to pick out the color of her choice.

While the furnishings in Mom's room were to her liking, I felt that a sprinkle of her own treasurers was necessary to connect her to the past. I knew this because of a sad story I once heard about a former neighbor of mine.

It seems that the neighbor and her husband went to Florida to live after he retired. They sold *everything* and took off. Their only child remained behind. Within two years, the wife was dead. Her daughter said she thought her mom died from loneliness. "Dad played golf every day to fill his hours, but Mom found nothing to replace the void. No tangible connection to the past existed."

With that memory in mind, I held back a few things from the auction I had shortly after Dad's death: the paintings Mom had done thirty years earlier, her cup-and-saucer collection, a chair that she had caned, family photos, and a television set. Her eyes lit up when she saw each and every item.

Having a room with a big window facing the parking lot was a blessing. The see-through lace curtain hung there just waiting for someone to peek through it. And Mom often did.

I would come into the room and find her sitting on the edge of the bed looking out the window. I would plop down and stare for a while with her.

"Look at that cute guy out there," she would say sheepishly, "I wonder where *he* belongs?" Or, "Look at that fat gal. She needs to lose fifty pounds." We would giggle and hug like a couple of high school girls.

Those were the early, better times before dementia really began to take its toll.

CHAPTER 16

THE CONDITIONING

ARLY ON, I ate with Mom and her tablemates a couple of times a week. It was a good way to pass the time because two-way conversations with her were now sporadic.

In addition, I learned a few things in the presence of other residents and staff members while sitting among them, such as the idea that dementia patients need routine in their lives. "It makes them feel safe," a nurse's aide said.

She quickly added, "That's why your mom has this special table at mealtime. She sits with the same people every day and eats at the same time every day."

Shortly after Mom's arrival she made the *grave* mistake of sitting on the wrong side of the table. She sat at Glenna's coveted spot. Glenna, an early Alzheimer resident, got into Mom's face, "You're in my seat. Move!"

It seems that Glenna had been a resident there for four years and coveted that particular spot at the table. Everyone knew that except Mom.

The kitchen staff had hustled to console Mom as she stood up to leave the table, but to no avail. She stomped to her room. Glenna was reprimanded, but it didn't faze her. She just sat there smiling … enjoying her coveted spot.

I was not part of that episode and would never have known about it, since Mom had short-term memory loss, but an aide who was working that night told me about it the next day.

A funny thing happened after that fiasco. Out of the blue, once in a while, Mom would blurt, "I don't get on with one of my tablemates. I forget which one."

Seating arrangements in the lobby were similarly territorial. When I visited mom, I would find her in the same chair near the kitchen door, reading. Irene sat across from her; Belva and Eldon on one of the sofas; residents Beryl and Doris on the other. Seldom did the arrangement vary.

One day when I was sitting in the lobby with Mom, I heard some commotion nearby. It was Belva. "Get up from there," she demanded from one of the residents. "That's my spot and Eldon's," she said. Belva tightened her grip on the purse and leaned in toward the resident and repeated her request. The resident moved. Conditioning at its finest.

CHAPTER 17

THE REPETITIONS

I STILL THOUGHT it was a *good* thing to have permanently assigned tablemates, even after Mom's fiasco with Glenna. And even after an aide confided in me, "Glenna is a pain in the ass." The episode had apparently left Mom unscathed.

Shortly after the fiasco, however, I joined the foursome for lunch. I wanted to see for myself what was going on among the tablemates, if anything.

Glenna took center stage. She babbled through the entire luncheon. "Why are we eating so early? Why do they give us so much food?" she asked over and over again. I knew from being around Alzheimer patients in the past that repetition was one symptom of the disease. I knew, too, that reminding Glenna that she had already asked those questions was futile.

"There's too much chicken here. I don't know why they give us so much," she whined as she shoved her carrots and mashed potatoes around the plate. "And why are we eating so early?" Tablemate Carrie looked at her watch every time Glenna asked that question and said, "It's not early, it's our regular time."

Good old Carrie. She seemed to go with the flow. I, on the other hand, was becoming increasingly impatient listening to the repetitions.

Just then, Glenna picked up her knife, cut into her chicken breast, and mumbled once more, "I don't know why they give us so much," then looked up at me. "I'm a picky eater, you know."

I tried to be patient, but found myself wanting the meal to be over. I changed the subject. "Glenna, I see you have a Coke there; you seem to enjoy that." I was calm and gentle.

"Oh yes," she smiled, "My son sees to it that I have a good supply. I keep them in the refrigerator in my room."

Mom had not said a word the entire dinner hour, but seemed happy merely sitting there cutting up her meat, salting her carrots, and buttering her roll. Same with Carrie.

The fourth tablemate, Lena, sat leaning to one side of her wheelchair, eating only when reminded. When she talked, which was seldom, her words were slurred. Glenna continued to mumble the same sentences over and over until the end of the meal.

The over-all experience gave me insight into the inner workings of Glenna and the challenges that face caregivers of other Alzheimer's patients.

THE WHISTLES

I WAS STUNNED one day when a staff member confided, "Did you know your mom is going to be a model in our style show?" Whoa!! My mom, who perpetually kept her light under a bushel? No way.

Yet, the executive director assured me it was true. Karen drove up from Cincinnati for the big day because she couldn't believe it either.

We sat in the large dining room filled with residents and friends, the sun brightly shining through the large windows, like spotlights. Each table had a small vase of fresh flowers to add to the ambience. We could see two of the models standing in line outside the doorway, grinning and waiting for their fifteen minutes of fame.

The narrator read the name of each model as she entered the room, then gave a description of the outfit. The models' faces radiated pride, testimony that senior citizens need not be overlooked or undervalued at this stage of their lives.

THE DEMENTIA DANCE

When Mom's name was read, she was the most radiant—a star among stars. She looked stunning in her size 12 black, ankle-length cocktail dress with pink trim, grinning from ear to ear as she shoved her walker along in front of her.

Ten residents had been chosen to model that day. Some wore suits and hats; some wore dressy dresses; a few wore casual attire, one wore warm-ups. All from a nearby consignment shop. It was a scene to behold! A style show with senior women—mostly in their eighties—some with walkers. Their hair was styled, makeup applied, and outfits selected to match each model's type. They were adorable. The notion that folks in assisted-living facilities could embrace life with such gusto tugged at my heartstrings.

Those in the audience of forty or so—staff, residents, and guests—applauded wildly. Most vocal were the half a dozen or so male residents who scoffed at the idea of taking part in a style show.

Afterwards, Mom sat down at the table where my sister and I sat, leaned in, and whispered, "I heard a couple of whistles when I walked by!" Her eyes danced.

We were thankful that she had agreed to model. Had Dad been there, he would have forbidden it. He believed a person shouldn't be in the public eye like that. What he meant was that he didn't want anyone else ogling over *his* pretty lady. He had always tried to keep her light under a bushel. One of those "keep 'em barefoot and pregnant" kind of guys. But Mom? She was game.

God love Karen. She had purchased the dress in case an occasion would arise for Mom to wear it.

THE GREETINGS

MOM WAS EXCITED to see me every single time I visited. That is, until the last two weeks of her life.

The greetings varied. I remember her sitting straight up in her lounge chair, eyes wide open, a big smile on her face. "How did you find me?" she asked. Sometimes it would be, "I *thought* you might be here today." And sometimes, "Well, for heaven's sake, look who's here!" Each time I wondered what prompted those comments.

My responses depended on the greeting. When she asked how I found her, I would laugh and say, "I pay your bills, so I know where you live," or "I saw your address in the church bulletin." Once, I leaned in as close as possible to her face and whispered, "Mom, I know everything. You know that. Just like you." She would look at me critically, then laugh.

One time I went to see her and the nurse said, "She's not feeling well. She's in her room."

I hurried down the hall and knocked on the door. No answer. I peeked in and found her lying on top of the covers. She was wearing jeans and that same cardigan my sister had given her. I sighed from relief that she was, at least, dressed.

She looked up, surprised, and said, "Well, for heaven's sake, I didn't expect to see you today."

Again, I wondered what thought process brought her to that conclusion, instead of, "Well, I thought you might be here today."

Later on, when trips to the hospital became frequent, she still greeted me with a smile. If I asked her if she knew who I was, she would smile and take my hand. "Of course I do," she said knowingly. I didn't press it, even though she didn't say my name.

On the second hospital stay, I crept into the dark, quiet room, not knowing whether she was asleep or awake. "Hi Mom," I whispered, leaning down to give her a kiss. She opened her eyes, grabbed my hands and said, tearfully, "Oh Rosemary, I love you so much."

Never in my life had I heard that from her. She had often said "love ya," but never gave an out-and-out declaration of her love like that before. It was the best greeting of all.

CHAPTER 20

THE GOODBYES

THE GOODBYES WERE not a problem for me. I felt strongly that Mom needed interaction with the residents and staff, so leaving Colony Court after my visits was guilt-free. Plus, I had another life which was equally important to me—a husband, children, grandchildren, friends, and clubs I belonged to.

I found that a good time to visit was the hour prior to dinnertime. I could at least get a reading on how she was doing; how she looked, how she behaved, was there any change in her condition. The dinnertime announcement was my cue to leave. Mom was usually okay with that.

Once in a while, however, she would ask, "Aren't you going to stay and eat with me?" Once in a while, I did.

I learned quickly, however, how to console her. She always said that the way to a man's heart was through his stomach, so when I responded with, "Mom, it's time to fix dinner for John," she would smile and say, "Oh yes, John needs his dinner. Such a nice-looking man, too."

If Mom was sitting in the lobby when I left, I would walk out the door, peek through the windowpanes, and wave to her. She would smile and wave back.

That simple gesture felt good. It was as if she were telling me, "Everything is okay, Rosemary. I am fine. Come back and see me. I'll still be here waiting for you." And I was telling her, "Not to worry, Mom, I'll be back."

I recall one goodbye that particularly touched my heart. Mom was sitting on the front porch with six other residents, enjoying the warmth of the sun. I had been pulling weeds near the front entrance, less than ten feet from the group.

Early on I had made myself the token gardener of the facility, using that job as another way to connect with Mom and the other residents.

It was resident Glenna's job to gather the weeds that I pulled and to stuff them into a paper bag; Anna's, to sweep the walk; Mom's, to *supervise!* She would stand on the sidewalk and point to the weeds I had missed. Good ol' Mom, the perfectionist.

On one of those days, after picking up my trowel, broom, and paper bag of weeds, I gave Mom a kiss and bid everyone adieu. Halfway to the car, I heard Mom brag, "That's my daughter, ya' know … the one that pulls the weeds and plants the flowers. She's my firstborn."

Those few words were music to my ears.

CHAPTER 21

THE ADVOCATE

AT THE OUTSET I became an advocate for Mom. If you can't be one, find one.

It's important to let the staff know you are on top of your game. Watch, listen, learn. Ask questions. Hold everyone accountable.

From the beginning I made sure the staff, residents, even guests at Colony Court knew my name and knew I was there to support my mom. I learned everyone's name and made it a point to interact with the nursing staff, kitchen help, and administration. I became a "watchdog."

I suggest visiting at different times of the day if you are able, to get a feel for the staff and place. I made it a point to visit at 10:00 or 11:00 in the morning or 3:00 in the afternoon—the hours preceding lunch and dinner. Sometimes I went after dinner if my day was filled with errands.

Mainly I wanted to make sure Mom was eating. Also, I was curious as to *what* she was eating. I had no complaints. *Her* only complaint was, "If I were doing the cooking, Rosemary, I would add a little more seasoning."

Visits at 8:00 A.M. were rare for me. Like Mom, I liked to sleep in, so I wasn't surprised to find her in bed the two times I did visit at that hour.

I asked the aide who was in her room why Mom wasn't up yet and did she usually eat breakfast. "Sometimes she gets up early enough to eat and sometimes she doesn't," she said. The aide and I discussed the pros and cons of it and agreed that breakfast was not all that important for Mom. Lunch and dinner, however, were not negotiable.

The times I went after dinner gave me a feeling of peace. On each occasion Mom was sitting in the lobby with half a dozen other residents. They were chatting or reading the paper.

The nursing staff distributed meds and snacks of pudding, chips, popcorn, and lemonade during that hour, all the while joking among the residents.

Saturdays and Sundays were quiet. Pet therapy, afternoon movies, church services, and the Sunday paper. Weekend visitors filed in and out. I stayed home.

There is a fine line between being an advocate and a nuisance, folks. It's okay to be both.

CHAPTER 22

THE CAMARADERIE

I FOUND A unique camaraderie among the residents. While I never heard them call one another by name, their gestures and body language said it all.

Betty, a dementia resident who babbled words no one could understand, was one of the most loving residents at Colony Court. Every time she saw me she threw up her arms, gave me a hug and a pat on the hand, beaming all the while. It didn't matter that she didn't make sense when she talked, or that she spent most of her time walking around aimlessly. Everyone loved her spirit.

On the other hand there was Ellie, a three-hundred-pound resident who threw her weight around like a bull in a china shop. While sitting in the lobby with Mom one day, I saw her shove resident Irene toward a chair four feet away because she was in her way.

Quick as a wink, another resident grabbed Irene before she could fall. Those seated nearby flocked to comfort her.

I was surprised by the residents' quick reactions. It gave me comfort to know they felt protective of one another.

I watched partially-blind Paul hand his tablemates salt and pepper before they asked for it. I saw him motion to a staff member for another glass of milk for a tablemate who had toppled his glass over. I noticed that he attempted to wipe up the spilled milk.

That same type of caring was displayed during crafts. The activities director would corral the residents into the activity room, pass out the items for the day's project, and give directions.

I watched in wonder as the women worked diligently on their crafts while craning their necks to see who needed assistance arranging, pasting, etc. "Here, that would look nice here, don't you think, Honey?" Or, "Does anyone need yellow beads? Red? Green? Blue?" They worked in tandem. It reminded me of the Seven Dwarfs—each following one another. Hi ho, hi ho.

CHAPTER 23

THE SUPPORT

THERE IS NO need to go it alone. Swallow your pride and reach out for help. It's not always an easy thing to do, but it gets easier over time.

It took a personal setback late in my life to realize it was okay to ask for help. Prior to that personal setback, I actually hadn't needed anyone else's help. But when I became a single parent, my prior independence and self-sufficiency crumbled. I fell flat on my face before reaching out to others for help. What a welcome surprise to learn that most people are ready and willing to help a friend in need.

My siblings willingly came to visit. Their children, grandchildren, and mine all came. Aunts, uncles and cousins did too.

I knew conversation would be awkward at the beginning of those visits, so a rule of thumb was for Mom to first give a quick tour of the facility. It broke the ice.

Her eyes lit up every time the family showed up. She especially enjoyed the little ones. The little girls would jump onto Mom's lap and let her read to them. The young boys had other ideas. They would rather run around the room or the facility. She loved their energy.

Pastor Bill from our hometown visited twice. She adored him, and so did I. I made it quite clear to my husband and parents that I had a schoolgirl crush on him. He was not only a "hunk," but a caring loving pastor with considerable charm. I tried not to drool in his presence.

The first time he visited Mom he came unannounced. It just so happened that I, too, came unannounced. There he was, sitting at a dining room table with Mom. My heart raced as I hurried to the greet him … oops, I mean them.

"Look who's here," Mom shouted, "It's about time, too!"

She was right, of course, because it had been a couple of months, but still—there he was. It tickled me that Mom felt comfortable enough around Pastor Bill to tease him. He apparently slipped under the radar of her short-term memory loss.

Volunteers from the local church stopped in weekly to pray with Mom. The Sunday school class from her hometown mailed a church bulletin to her every week. Each member wrote a personal note on the front page. Mom cherished those bulletins and carried them in the basket of her walker.

Residents and staff at Colony Court also helped. More than once I found the secretary sitting in the lobby with Mom, reading to her from a magazine. In my absence, aides sometimes took the time to comb Mom's hair and put makeup on her.

For two weeks before Mom's death, hospice workers were there for her and me.

CHAPTER 24

THE REMARKS

IN ORDER TO deal with the inevitable stress which escalates as your loved one's condition deteriorates, you need skills. They are not easy to come by.

I did not find them in the seminars I attended or the books that I read. I did not find them by talking with other people. I found them by trial and error. The largest, most looming fact was that you and I must go where the residents are in *their* minds, not ours.

For example, denying that there was a man in Aunt Jane's room the night before, when Aunt Jane said there *was,* is counter-productive. Instead, ask Aunt Jane to tell you about it. I know it sounds dumb and feels awkward, but with patience and perseverance it can be done.

Ethel is another good example of going where the resident "is." From the lobby I heard "I need your help" from Ethel as she stood at Director Dee's desk wringing her hands.

"What's the matter?" asked Dee.

"I don't know what to do. Help me," she cried, "I've lost January."

Because of Dee's expertise with deftly handling her charges, she stood up and walked around her desk to where Ethel was standing. She took her arm. Together, they headed to Ethel's room.

She later told us that Ethel had flipped over the December page of her calendar and found nothing there and got confused.

The secretary told me the following day that her husband had gone out as soon as he heard the calendar story and bought a new one for her to take to Ethel. The secretary's eyes teared up as she spoke.

Another example is resident Beryl. She grabbed me one day in the hallway and asked, "Do you have my clothes?"

Instead of answering, I asked, "Do you think they might be in your closet?"

Modeling Executive Dee's behavior, I took Beryl's arm and guided her to her room. Together we checked the closet. Plenty of clothes there! In fact, everything was lined up neat and tidy-like, as if Martha Stewart herself had been there.

"There they are, Beryl," I exclaimed and pointed to the row of hangers. Her eyes brightened and she threw her arms around me. I patted myself on the back. I was learning.

Resident Tom was in early stages of Alzheimer's, but it wasn't obvious to those who didn't know him. One evening when a small group of us was sitting on the front porch, he excused himself, saying, "Pardon me, folks, I'm going to call my son." He soon he came roaring out of the building, "Well, it's a helluva thing to learn through a phone call that your wife is dead!"

It was common knowledge around the place that Tom's wife had died a year or so earlier and that he was well aware of it, so I bit my tongue and didn't say anything. I had learned to go where Tom was at the moment.

He was quiet for a while, then said, "Or … maybe I just forgot. I do that sometimes." He added, "I know she got tired of taking care of me. Maybe that's what killed her." He turned to me and asked, "Do you smoke?" Tom had moved on, and I was still learning.

CHAPTER 25

THE LAUGHS

ON OCCASION, COLONY Court could be called a Comedy Club. One-liners from residents came at unexpected times and kept everyone within earshot entertained. Whether intentional or not, those one-liners kept things lively.

For instance, Glenna, a lobby-sitter resident, kept us in stitches with her ongoing sagas. She once said of her former husband, "I haven't seen my husband in twenty years. I got fed up with his bullying, so one day I just up and walked right out the front door, down that long driveway and out of his life. I never looked back." She paused and added, "Serves him right, the no-good deadbeat!" Everyone howled.

My own mom cracked me up every now and then. When I told her that my best high school chum was coming to town for our fifty-year high school class reunion, she leaned in and whispered, "Does Shirley know you're old?"

On another occasion, Mom had wandered off to a building near the Colony. When I walked up for my daily visit, one of the residents said, "Your Mom's not here." Stunned, I questioned her, "What do you mean she's not here?" She stood up and pointed in the direction of a large housing unit. It was close enough that I could see Mom sitting among three other ladies on a concrete patio. I was still in shock that she had walked off without the staff's knowledge, but I did not panic. Instead, I watched and waited.

Within minutes an older lady came walking toward Colony, arm in arm with Mom. "Does anyone know this woman? She says her name is Lois and that she is from Mt. Gilead."

"That's right," I said, "Thanks for bringing her back." I looked at Mom and asked, "Where have you been, Kiddo?" With a wide grin and bright eyes, she responded, "Oh, I've been to church!"

One day during craft hour, I sat with Mom in an effort to help her color a page with clowns on it. There were a dozen of us around two tables with a large bowl of Magic Markers in the middle of each one. Residents were tossing them in and out of the bowls as needed. Except Roxie.

The activities director leaned over Roxie's shoulder and asked, "Why aren't you coloring, Roxie?"

Roxie turned, looked up at her and replied, "I can't use these markers. They're for left-handed people."

One of the residents asked ninety-eight-year-old Audrey if she was ready to go into the dining room for dinner, and Audrey responded, "Oh no, I can't do that. My mother is coming by this afternoon."

Elsie, an Alzheimer resident, reached out for me in the lobby one day and whispered, "Did you get invited to the party?"

I looked at her, searching for a response, then simply replied, "No, did you?"

She sat back in her wheelchair, squinted, and responded, "No."

I leaned into her and whispered, "I'll find out who *is* invited and let you know. Okay?" She nodded, winked and gave me a high five. It felt like high school all over again.

Some of those dear folks passed away while I was there for Mom. A few were sent to nursing homes or shuttled to other facilities. But make no mistake. They all left an imprint on those of us who were left behind. Their individuality, charm, and wit were priceless.

CHAPTER 26

THE GIRLS

I T WAS PARTY time when my sister came for a visit at Colony once every month. It felt terrific with just us girls. When Dad was alive we included him in our outings, but now, with just the three of us, it felt oh so good. Dad had always seemed anxious to get back home.

Karen was fun. Mom would often say, "Karen has such a happy look about her." And when Karen was there, I didn't have to figure out when to go visit, what to do during that time, or what to say.

Karen and I worked out a system. Since Mom loved drugstores, we would drive to the local CVS for a few personal items she needed: Ponds cleanser, Maybelline eyeliner, Jergens hand lotion—brand names she was familiar with. She spent most of the time there, however, reading birthday cards. That was her comfort zone. She never forgot a birthday. Until dementia set in, that is.

Part of the ritual was to eat out. We liked the Longhorn Steak House where Mom could have her favorite, liver and onions. Even though she simply stared at the menu, we made sure the waitress gave her one anyway. We would eventually suggest, "How about liver and onions today, Mom?" She would quickly close her menu, nod and smile.

Upon returning to Colony, I would fix a pot of coffee or tea to enjoy with the cookies Karen had stashed in her tote. She couldn't help herself. She loved treats.

Karen also brought photos of her family for Mom to see. Often we would get out the many photos and cards Mom had received and remind her who everyone was and how much people loved her. "Oh, those aren't all mine, are they?" she would ask in amazement.

When Mom's condition deteriorated to the place where she could no longer eat solids, one of us would feed her at her bedside. Instead of liver and onions, it was mashed potatoes, smashed peas, and pudding. Mom didn't seem to mind—she enjoyed whatever was put in front of her.

Eventually, when she was reduced to drinking water from a straw, we still helped. The staff showed us how to mix a special thickener with her water, which somehow kept her from choking.

Until the very end, we massaged her arms, legs, and face with moisturizing cream. We also combed her hair, drew on her eyebrows, applied blush and lipstick as if everything were normal.

"Girls Day" was a special day for me to look forward to. Lots of laughs, hugs and kisses.

CHAPTER 27

THE MEMORY LOSS

I HAD TO get used to Mom's questions: "Where am I? Is this my room? How did you find me?" They were ongoing reminders that Mom's short-term memory loss was there to stay and I'd better learn to deal with it.

Earlier, I had heard friends say in disbelief, "Can you believe my mother? She said I haven't been to see her in ages, and I was just there yesterday!" I sympathized, but didn't fully grasp the gravity of it until Mom said the same thing about me, and I visited nearly every day.

Because of Mom's syncope (a condition where the blood pressure drops when a person stands up), she needed a walker to help keep her steady. But with her short-term memory loss she forgot to use it.

No matter how often therapists and nurse's aides reminded her, she forgot. I also reminded her. When I did, she would look at me like a child who had been reprimanded and say, "Oh yes. They want me to use it all the time, don't they?"

It bothered me that the interns and other staff members who worked in the kitchen didn't have sufficient training or experience with dementia residents with short-term memory loss. Young interns would set a glass of water in front of the residents at meal time and say sweetly, "Now be sure to drink your water" and move on.

"That's not gonna happen, Girlfriend," I would say under my breath. Short-term memory loss precludes that. In retrospect, I could have helped by confronting the student or telling the executive director.

Instead, when I had lunch or dinner with Mom, I would hand her the glass of water and she would drink it down with gusto. Otherwise, it would have gone untouched. I mention the water situation because it is quite common for older folks to become dehydrated, necessitating a call to 911.

Mom gradually began to neglect her personal habits. Forgetting to brush her teeth was one of them. When I was there I simply asked if she had remembered to brush. She would wrinkle her forehead, purse her lips and say, "I don't know." The solution was an easy one.

"Mom, you'll want to brush your teeth before you go out to the lobby," I would say, and she did it. Without prompting, however, it would never have happened.

She would soon forget that the special crafts she made earlier in the activity room were made by her. "I don't know where those pretty pictures came from. Aren't they pretty?" were her responses when she spied them on her corkboard. She seemed surprised when I reminded her that she had made them.

Refrigerated items such as yogurt, puddings, and bottled water we took to Mom all went begging. Reminding her that they were there for her use fell on deaf ears. Eventually we stopped taking them.

When I saw that Mom was not flushing the toilet anymore I flushed it for her and chalked it up to her memory loss instead of carelessness.

Try not to get mad when your loved one doesn't follow through with something you had agreed upon. When I washed the few dishes we had used in her room, she would holler, "Rosemary, don't worry about those dishes. Leave them in the sink. I'll get to them later." She never did.

We were lucky, very lucky, with Mom and her dementia. She was perky, easy to manage, even-tempered, healthy physically, content, and always glad to see us.

CHAPTER 28

THE MISSING ITEMS

MY HUSBAND WARNED me. Don't take valu-
ables to an assisted-living facility, nursing home, or
extended care facility. "I know what I'm talking about,"
he assured me, "Someone stole my Dad's false teeth!"

It struck me as funny, so I laughed out loud, but
soon found out the severity of it when Mom misplaced
her glasses.

"Has anyone seen my mom's glasses?" I asked,
standing in the middle of the lobby at Colony Court. A
couple of the residents lifted up couch pillows to check,
but found nothing.

I had already searched Mom's room: the wastebasket,
drawers, shelves in the bathroom, her purse. The thought
of using my time and energy to get new ones rankled
me. Would she simply lose them again? She had recently
misplaced her hearing aids. I'd searched high and low
for them and asked the staff to help in my search. I

eventually found them in her wastebasket under a napkin in a used paper cup.

When Director Dee came out of her office, I told her the situation with the glasses.

"H-m-m-m-m," she pondered, "I don't know. We'll keep an eye out for them."

They'll keep an eye out for them? What did that mean? I asked myself. Her response felt more like a dismissal than a sincere commitment to find Mom's glasses.

Dee hadn't gotten three feet away from me when she whirled around. "I've got an idea," she said with confidence. "Come with me."

We headed down the hall to the room of resident Pearl. "You stay here. I'll go in," Dee winked. She knocked and no one came to the door, so she used her master key and disappeared into the room. Within minutes, she reappeared with a pair of glasses in her hand. "Are these your mom's?" she asked. They were.

Dee explained, "Pearl takes things once in a while and puts them in her room. She doesn't even know she does it."

When Mom was in Selby Center, the rehab facility where she stayed for twenty days after a hospital stint, her clothes were often missing. Even though I had taped up a large sign "Daughter Will Do the Laundry" above the laundry basket, it was ignored.

The first time it happened, I marched right down to the front desk to report the loss. The gal behind the desk casually replied, "Oh, these things happen, honey. Go to the laundry room down the hall and see if her things are there."

THE MISSING ITEMS

I hustled down the hall like a dog in heat. Peeking into the laundry room, I spied stacks and racks of clothes. The gal folding clothes yelled over the hum of the dryer, "Come on in. If you're looking for something in particular, it'll be on one of those racks." So they were.

I learned not to take anything of significant value to any hospital, rehab center, assisted-living facility, or long-term care complex. Better safe than sorry.

CHAPTER 29

THE BASICS

IT CAN COST a bundle to replace valuables that go missing. My advice is to do what successful coaches do: stick with the basics.

I finally learned that it didn't matter to Mom whether Karen and I took her to the Longhorn Steak House for liver and onions or to Bob Evans for homemade vegetable soup. She seemed happy either way.

It also didn't seem to matter whether we bought her a $3 sweater at a thrift shop or a $25 one at Macy's. She was content with everything we gave her.

We learned that discussions of the immediate past were lost on her. Only the present and the distant past were intact.

"This vegetable soup has barley in it. I used to make vegetable soup, but I added beef to mine." Bingo! She was on the money with those remarks. But if I asked her what she had for lunch when we got back to her room, she wouldn't know.

She knew she had painted the hangings on her living room wall. "I painted that picture hanging up there, didn't I?" she asked proudly.

I would engage her in talk about family and friends we both had known long ago. It was like a refresher course for me on our family history, and it gave her a chance to reminisce. I considered it "quality time."

We would look at magazines and the hometown newspaper together, finding names and tidbits we could share.

We would leaf through the two baskets of photos and cards from family and friends. Over and over. It reminded me of when I read to my children and they would beg, "Read it again. Read it again!"

I remember watching Mom study a photo of her standing next to the headstone of her and dad at the cemetery. Plainly etched on Dad's side were the dates of his birth and death, hers with date of birth only. The only comment she made was, "Look how pretty I look in that pink sweater."

Photos, magazines, inexpensive gifts, the sharing of the present and past worked for us. It kept things simple and kept costs to a minimum. Paying the monthly rent was costly enough.

CHAPTER 30

THE FALLS

IT WAS IN October of Mom's second year at Colony, her fourth year into dementia, that falls became the order of the day.

With her short-term memory loss, she would forget to use her walker. During the day, someone was there to remind her of it, but at night she was on her own.

The first fall was at night between her bed and a nearby chair. An aide found her while making her morning rounds. There did not appear to be any damage, but the staff notified me about it anyway.

The very next night, the second fall occurred. The same aide found her lying at the end of the bed, a two-inch gash on her forehead. Apparently she had smacked it on a nearby baseboard.

The squad was called and got there before I did. They told the staff, "She knows her name and where she lives. We've bandaged her up. She should be okay."

But she was *not* okay and was never the same after that second fall.

The very next day she fell again. This time the fall did not warrant a call to the squad. Just me.

The staff and I suspected that Mom's falls were due to a failed attempt to reach the bathroom without her walker. The room was equipped with a call button and cord at the head of her bed, but with short-term memory loss she could not remember to use it.

Things were getting dicey now and I was increasingly frightened. It was getting hard not to cry while talking about or with Mom. Dementia was taking its toll.

CHAPTER 31

THE 911s

THE FIRST TIME Mom complained about not feeling well, I was sitting in the lobby with her. This was early in her stay at Colony.

"Lois, where does it hurt?" the nurse asked. Mom just sat there with a grimace. The nurse continued with, "Is it your stomach?" No response. "Your chest?" No response. "Your abdomen?" No response. "I can't help you unless I know where you hurt. Where does it hurt? Tell me," she said firmly.

Come on, Mom, tell her, I yelled to myself, as if that would help.

Mom finally pointed to her chest area. "I just feel funny in here," she said.

The nurse, thinking it could be a heart attack, called 911. "Better to be safe than sorry," she said. Mom's pain was eventually diagnosed as acid reflux.

I realized for the first time that getting accurate information from dementia patients when they are in pain is difficult, if not impossible. This is one area where an advocate is vital.

The second 911 call was a few weeks later. Again, Mom was in the lobby. She had fainted, her vital signs barely visible. The staff was faithful in their calls to me, letting me know when these events occurred and what their plan was.

"Nothing major is wrong with your mom," the emergency room doctor told me. "She has a urinary tract infection." He went on to say that urinary tract infections are common among older folks. I didn't know.

One physician, after another of her falls, prescribed physical therapy to strengthen her feet and legs and build her confidence when she used her walker. In addition, she would be taught how to safely get out of bed, chairs and sofas to help eliminate potential falls.

Physical therapy meant a rehab center, which meant a change of facility, which meant taking Mom out of her comfort zone. Would she be able to handle it? Would I?

I left the hospital with a lengthy list of rehabilitation centers. I was on my own. Heaven help me.

THE JOKE

BEFORE MOM LEFT the hospital for rehab, the doctor suggested she wear support hose, those stark white knee sox worn to help with circulation. He ordered a pair for her on the spot.

"Okay," I mused, "Exactly how will this work with someone who has dementia and cannot even remember to flush the toilet?" To ask Mom to attempt something as complicated as putting on support hose seemed ludicrous.

In theory it should work, but I knew from experience that it most certainly would not. Reality trumps theory every time.

When I was a fledgling speech-and-hearing therapist, I wrote my trusty lesson plans, just as I was taught to. However, when I was assigned a school in a low-income area, I found it necessary to chuck those plans.

One frisky little six-year-old girl did not know her phone number, address, or last name. "Whoa, this is not good," I thought, so I spent the first few weeks teaching her those basics. I incorporated her speech problems within my lesson plans and moved forward.

When the perky little therapist arrived and pulled the hose from a plastic bag, each was the size of a Hershey bar. I winced, thinking, "This will be v-e-r-y interesting."

"Perky" shared right off the bat that she was new at her job. I was pleased to see her proceed with gusto as if she were performing brain surgery!

She rolled the stark whites down to the toe with admirable determination and took hold of Mom's leg. She said, in her naiveté, "This shouldn't take very long, Mrs. Osborn." I could barely keep from laughing.

I knew it would take forever, because Mom had drop-dead good-looking legs, the ones with those sexy firmly shaped calves. And I knew those whites would not stretch over those calves without a severe meltdown on the part of both the therapist and Mom.

That poor girl took hold of Mom's foot and tried to pull the hose up over her size eights and over those hefty calves. She tugged and tugged and panted and groaned. Mom was grimacing in her effort to cooperate.

The therapist soon had one of her feet planted on the floor, the other dangling from the side of the bed where her knee was bent for leverage. She was leaning in and tugging as she toiled.

By now Mom's hospital gown was up around her throat and she was scrambling to keep it down while pushing to get her leg into that one white sock. She was also moaning, "How much longer?"

My heart went out to both of them. The therapist's face was streaked with sweat, ringlets stuck on her forehead. The poor thing was doing what she had been told to do.

I could contain myself no longer. I reached in and tapped Perky on the shoulder and laughed, "Do you really think that is going to work? It's taken you ten minutes to *almost* get one of those support hose *almost* over one of Mom's calves."

She stopped on a dime. I stepped back for fear she might slug me. Instead, she laughed. "Not really," she said.

Breathing a sigh of relief, she called for the doctor.

Within minutes he was in the room. After the therapist told him of her dilemma, he looked straight and hard at me. "All right," he said, "She won't have to wear them. We'll find another way." Advocates at work.

CHAPTER 33

THE VISITS

MOM LIKED IT at the rehabilitation center, and so did I. The executive director was playing "Moon River" on a white, baby grand piano when I first visited the facility. A handful of smiling residents sat on a nearby sofa watching and listening.

Not only did the facility have a welcoming reception area, it was also a mere fifteen minutes from Colony. Selby was clean and the staff friendly. I was sold on the spot.

Mom especially liked the fact that she had a roommate. "She doesn't talk much, but she's a nice lady. The poor thing has a tube down her throat," Mom said.

I went to see Mom every day at Selby to find out how she was faring and get the lay of the land. Karen visited, bringing her awesome chocolate chip cookies.

Director Dee, secretary Brenda, and a nurse from Colony Court also visited with flowers and candy.

Mom's eyes lit up when she saw them—and the gifts! I was surprised and thankful that they would take time from their busy schedules to spend time with her.

Mom's favorite thing to do at Selby was to sit in an overstuffed chair in the "lockdown" unit with the Alzheimer's patients. She would lean in and whisper to me, "Look at that poor woman holding a doll baby. Do you think *she* thinks it's real?" Or, "You know, that man makes no sense whatsoever when he talks. But, he's nice-looking, isn't he?" I was thrilled that she was alert enough to differentiate among the folks in the unit.

I was happy to be with her when she took part in the activities, answering nearly every trivia question, knowing the names of every song during the sing-alongs. She wouldn't yell out the answers like boisterous Bill and Monty did, but I could hear her. And I was proud.

When it was time to leave Selby, I met with a team of specialists. They said Mom was doing as well as could be expected, but stressed that she could no longer process information as she had in the past. The physical therapist gave me an example. "I have to lift her leg to get her started on leg lifts. If I merely say, 'Lift your leg, Lois,' she can't do it on her own." It reminded me of the glass of water that she wouldn't drink unless she was prompted.

I had spent two weeks witnessing staff members reach out to my mom and their other charges in a kind and caring way. They treated everyone with dignity. I left Selby with a happy heart.

DOSES OF DIGNITY

IT WAS THE dignity that touched my heart. Situations arose over and over where staff members had a choice to respond defensively or with dignity. They chose the latter.

The first day I was there, I heard a soft voice speak. "Is there anything else we can do for you, Doctor?" I turned to see a well-dressed older woman in a black, wide-brimmed hat kneeling beside a wheelchair; a tall young man behind her.

The doctor fussed with a blanket on his lap and smiled. "No, I don't think so. I'm all right." The woman stood up, gave the doctor a kiss on the cheek and patted him on the shoulders. The young man took hold of the wheelchair. "It's time to go to your room, Grandpa," he said. I could barely hold back the tears. The whole scene screamed "dignity."

Within minutes, I heard an agitated voice. "Someone needs to get rid of those dogs! Just look at them. They're all over the place." It was from a female, staring out a nearby window. She was wringing her hands and shaking her head.

A nurse rushed to her side knowing there were no dogs. "Ruthie, the staff will get rid of those dogs for us. Would you like that?"

Ruthie looked at the nurse, then at the window, then back at the nurse. "Okay," she finally said softly, and slipped her hands through the nurse's arm. That scene also screamed dignity.

Those were just two of the many displays of tenderness I witnessed while Mom was there. There were many more.

While staff members worked their magic, I learned the art of dealing with those who have Alzheimer's and other forms of dementia.

It did not seem to matter whether the residents were male or female, educated or uneducated, docile or outrageous. It did not seem to matter whether they were homemakers, truck drivers or shop owners. All were treated with dignity.

In the dining room, I watched Ginny, a mother of ten, defy the nurses by throwing her pills across the room or dropping them into her tablemate's water glass. She would clamp her lips shut until the nurses left. I watched the nurses crush up the pills behind Ginny's back and stick them into her pudding or ice cream when she wasn't looking. She ate them unwittingly.

I watched the residents as they laughed and tossed their dinner rolls to Tom. "I used to teach high school math," he said proudly, "But now I feed the birds. I can see them from my window." He went on, "The folks here give me their bread every day." I followed suit. Mom ate hers.

From the lounge, I watched Mary, a former WAC in World War II, flail her arms as she hurled obscenities at one of the other residents. It was a short-lived tantrum, over before a nurse could respond. The residents didn't even seem to notice or care.

I watched Clara, a one-time manager of an upscale dress shop, sit day after day in the lounge, simply staring; Helen, a former homemaker, crying and softly calling over and over, "Mama;" and Victor, a one-time truck driver, jabbering on and on. It didn't seem to matter that no one was listening.

I watched the staff weave in and out of the lounge talking, teasing, and tending to those and other residents; calling them by name, patting them on the shoulders, holding their hands, or whispering to them as if they were sharing secrets.

The one place they didn't have to tend to them was during the Friday sing-alongs. It was there where the residents came to life. The scene reminded me of the movie *Awakenings*, a powerful true story of a maverick doctor and the patients whose lives he changed through the use of an experimental drug to "awaken" them from their catatonic states. It worked. But, only for a short period of time.

I watched the residents as they clapped, tapped, and sang loudly and effortlessly as the pianist pounded out the oldies: "I Want A Girl Just Like the Girl that Married Dear Old Dad," "When You Wore a Tulip," and "Don't Fence Me In."

When the leader asked for suggestions of other favorites, a chorus of shouts would ring out: "Hang on Sloopy," "When the Roll is Called Up Yonder," "God Bless America," and others. More clapping, tapping, and singing. I couldn't believe my eyes … or ears. Music had "awakened" them. But, as in the movie *Awakenings,* only for a short period of time.

My mom, of course, did not remember her stay at Selby. But I will not soon forget the Claras, the Marys, and the doctors who live with Alzheimer's on a daily basis.

Nor will I forget the staff members who cared for them. They gave each and every one what every human being wants and deserves. Dignity.

CHAPTER 35

THE DOWNTURN

AFTER THAT SECOND fall, Mom's condition took a dramatic downturn. She no longer dressed herself without help. She no longer interacted with other residents. She was confined to a wheelchair. The twinkle in her eyes was gone.

The greeting, "How did you find me?" and the waving goodbye through the window panes became history.

"Oh, Ro," she began to mumble over and over until I diverted her attention to something else. Periodically, however, she would shock me by coming out with something appropriate to the occasion.

One particular day when we were on a joy ride, she continued to mumble, "Oh, Ro, oh, Ro," then all of a sudden blurt, "It must be garbage day!" Trash cans and recycle bins lined the curbs. She later pointed to the sky and said, "Oh, Rosemary, look at all those clouds." Otherwise, she mumbled "Oh, Ro, oh, Ro."

I never learned from her what "Oh, Ro" meant, but one of the aides told me it was a term of endearment; that my mom was calling the first two letters of my name. "It's a sense of security for her," she added. I didn't believe it for a minute, but I stopped trying to figure it out.

On that same day I learned that she lost the capacity to remember the basics. When I got her to the car and tried to help her into the front seat, she just stood there. I retrieved the seatbelt and said, "Okay, Mom, go ahead and get in." She didn't move. By then, I was growing impatient.

Then it hit me. "Mom, do you remember *how* to sit down?" I asked, incredulously. She did not. Stunned, I reached behind her knees so they would bend and then slid her onto the seat. With tears in check, I reminded myself that this frustration, her moaning, her withdrawing were merely tests. Bigger ones would surely follow.

One of those bigger ones was her toilet habits. While she had stopped flushing long before, the process of sitting down on the toilet had become fearful for her. She wailed the entire time she was in the bathroom squatting, never completely sitting down on the toilet.

I wanted to hold her in my arms and let her cry until the tears were gone. I wanted to kiss her cheeks to reassure her that someone loved her.

Instead, I stood by helplessly, until I could do it no longer. The strain, the pain, the moans from her, the helplessness for me—it was too much.

I turned to the aides, who were trained to help those in Mom's condition, and they handled it beautifully and skillfully. I wondered how much longer it would be until she would have to leave Colony Court and go to a nursing home where she could get round-the-clock care.

In front of Mom I kept my head high. I thought of those thousands of others who were facing similar challenges, and it made me feel better. Not much, but a little.

CHAPTER 36

THE GUILT

WELCOME TO THE club if you feel pangs of guilt when dealing with your loved one. I've read many a book on the subject of guilt and learned that once you make amends for a transgression, the guilt is subsequently removed. Maybe so, but for me the guilt remains like chewing gum stuck to the bottom of my shoe.

For many years I felt guilty about not being able to "fix" things, mostly relationships, family squabbles. You'd think I would learn because, try as I may, I could never fix any of them.

A counselor once told me, "Of course you try to fix things. You are a firstborn and a female. The perfect criteria for trying to make things right. When you fail, guilt follows as night follows day.

THE GUILT

I felt guilty because I couldn't stop the downward spiraling of Mom's dementia. I felt I should be doing more. But what?

I even felt guilty when I couldn't "fix" the other residents at Colony. Now that's sick.

CHAPTER 37

THE EPISODE

PART OF MOM'S downturn resulted in an incident that neither my sister nor I will soon forget.

By now the holiday season was upon us, and Karen had come for her monthly visit, toting fresh fruit and chocolate chip cookies. What appeared to be a routine visit turned topsy-turvy.

We had just finished eating in the dining room and were in Mom's room enjoying the warmth of the sun shining through the lace curtain. Karen placed the fruit and cookies on a small platter and handed it to us. We ate with gusto.

Before we could finish our second round of cookies, Karen and I heard a gurgling sound from Mom's stomach. Mom stopped chewing and stared into space. Karen yelled, "Get the basket!"

I grabbed the one nearest to me and thrust it under Mom's chin. Just in the nick of time.

She upchucked some thick, strange looking stuff—the color of the cookies—the consistency of cookie dough—for what seemed like eons. The mass kept coming and coming … and coming.

Karen and I stared at each other in disbelief. After we regained our composure, I cried, "Whoa, Mom, no more cookies for you!" We couldn't help ourselves; we all laughed.

I called the nurse. She informed us that what had happened was normal for late-stage dementia. The stomach was not processing food as it should and formed a backup of sorts.

The words "late dementia" stung. The laughs between the girls would be fewer and farther between from now on. Heaven help us.

THE HEARTBREAK

THE NURSE WAS right about Mom's food not processing as it should. Not only was it not processing, Mom was now also eating very little of any food that was placed before her. More often than not she would simply sit there with her head down on her chest, fiddling with her handkerchiefs. Quiet. Sobbing.

Eating had always been the love of Mom's life. When she was a "clean-plater" at Colony, I would tease her, "Mom, the day you stop eating will be the day you are on your way out!" It was funny then, but not now.

God love the young staff members who were in training and serving the residents. I'm sure they were high on hopes for their jobs, yet they were low on experience.

I wanted to shout at them and shake my fist, "Can't you see that my mom needs attention more than anyone else in this room? Why isn't someone feeding her?"

Instead, I would feed her by cutting her meat into teeny bits before lifting them to her mouth and whispering to her how good it would taste. She would dutifully open up ever so slightly and take in a bite or two. It reminded me of a baby robin opening its beak for a morsel from its mother. More often than not, however, her lips were clamped together.

Ice cream and pudding were now her mainstays. Her tongue was out before I got the lid pried off the cartons. I felt triumphant when that happened. I took it as a sign that she would be okay.

Of course she wasn't going to be okay. She was going from bad to worse.

During lunch one day, an experienced aide told me that the inability to eat solid foods was one more sign that Mom was sliding quickly down that slippery slope of dementia.

Thank goodness I had my family to support me. It was too much to go it alone. Too much for one heart to handle.

"Rosemary, you know she is not going to get better—only worse," my husband kept reminding me. I knew he was right, yet this feeling of constant helplessness had me nearly paralyzed. How could I shake it?

CHAPTER 39

THE SOBBING

MOM'S SOBBING CONTINUED. Quietly and persistently. Head bent down, a handkerchief in her hand.

My heart ached for her, knowing that she would hate what was happening to her. In the past, she would often say, "I don't *ever* want to be a burden to anyone."

Each time I found her whimpering, I wanted to hold her in my arms and say, "It's okay, Mom, you're no bother to anyone. We're here with you because we want to be." Instead, I would simply take her hand and hold it.

Resident Viv was the first to point out Mom's sobbing. She grabbed me as I entered the lobby one morning and proceeded to show me what was going on. I say *show* because Viv's speech was slurred—barely recognizable—from a stroke she had experienced a few years earlier. Viv pointed to her eyes, ran a finger down her cheeks, then frowned and pointed toward Mom.

From then on it became common to find Mom slumped to one side of her chair, twisting one of her handkerchiefs, her chest heaving ever so slightly from whimpering. It reminded me of a puppy we once had that made the same sound when he needed someone to take him outside.

When I asked her what was wrong, she just sat there. I hugged her and said, "Tell me what's wrong, Mom." Again, no answer. Just sobbing.

One day shortly after that, I found secretary Brenda sitting with Mom on the sofa, showing her some photos from a *Reminisce* magazine. Mom had a frown on her face, but was looking down at the photos.

My heart skipped a beat. Mom was connecting with Brenda! And, Mom looked terrific! She was wearing her dressy black-and-white striped blouse with its satin collar and dressy black slacks over black flats. The hairdresser had curled her hair earlier in the day. I wondered, "How can someone who looks so chic be in such pain?"

I heard Brenda ask, "Lois, would you like me to keep reading to you?" Mom looked up *very* slowly and nodded, whimpering ever so softly. Brenda proceeded to flip through the magazine, commenting on the photos, "Lois, remember when you wore hairstyles and high heels like that?" Again, Mom nodded *very* slowly, still whimpering softly.

When Brenda finished with the magazine, I heard, "Lois, I'll see you later. Maybe we can look at more magazines then." I loved Brenda for her acts of kindness. She didn't *have* to read to Mom. It was out of the goodness of her heart that she did so. God is good.

CHAPTER 40

THE ENTERTAINMENT

EVEN THOUGH THE sad times were inevitable, Colony Court kept things lively. The activities director outdid herself by bringing in local talent at least once a week. A much-needed breath of fresh air during troubling times. She was a ray of sunshine.

She booked a professional violinist who roamed in between and around the tables after the dinner hour, charming residents and guests alike with her classical, pop, and Broadway tunes. She shared with us that, in her earlier life, she had played background to the Bee Gees when she was a member of the Columbus Symphony Orchestra.

The activities director booked a young tenor from a local opera house who bellowed from the activities room loud enough to hear him downtown. It was a blessing that many of the residents were hard-of-hearing.

Young school children helped with crafts and read to the residents. Their eyes lit up when young people were around.

There were music groups from churches. Singers and dancers from recreation centers strutted their stuff.

The Fourth of July celebrations were especially colorful. Handfuls of mini flags were placed in cups on the fireplace mantel, lined up like toy soldiers standing at attention. Additional mini flags were tucked into small clear glasses as centerpieces on the tables, and some were placed into a huge red, white, and blue Fourth of July cake. Patriotism at its finest.

The most precious memory I have of the festivities is the Christmas dinner and surprise visit from Santa the December before Mom died. A Christmas buffet was held, so I sat Mom down at a table for six and filled a dinner plate for her, plus a small plate with a piece of her favorite dessert, coconut cream pie.

After filling my own plates, I sat down and chatted with the person next to me. Out of the corner of my eye, I caught Mom poking her fork into my butterscotch pie. Her coconut cream pie was already gone!

"Hey, what's this about, Lady?" I teased, "Eating the food right out from under my nose when I'm not looking." Everyone at the table laughed, including Mom. I did not realize at the time that eating solid foods was becoming increasingly difficult for her.

That same night, when Santa boomed in with his boisterous "ho, ho, ho," Mom's eyes lit up like a Christmas tree. "What's your name, little girl?" he asked, heading toward Mom. After telling him, he reached into his bag of goodies. "Well, Lois, here's a little gift for you from Santa. Ho, ho, ho," he bellowed. She reached up and kissed him.

I don't even remember what was in the gift bag, but I do remember that the activities director took a picture of Mom with Santa. Her face glowed, her eyes sparkled. She did, in fact, look like a little girl. God bless her. And, God bless the activities director.

CHAPTER 41

THE SURPRISES

I REPEAT. GOD bless the activities director. And, God bless the rest of the staff at Colony. I was constantly amazed at the unexpected perks from them and the residents. There were too many to count, but here are a few.

Shortly after Mom got settled in at Colony, secretary Brenda would keep me informed of the events of the day. "Your mom was just humming away this morning as she read the newspaper," she offered cheerfully, and then went on to say that Mom had helped her stuff envelopes that afternoon. She continued, "She's doing great!" These comments were unsolicited. I love a friendly place!

The activities director often volunteered to tell me that Mom had been out with the residents on a trip to Frisch's for dessert or on a trip to the park. With Mom's short-term memory loss, I never would have known.

The nursing staff kept me informed of Mom's daily routine. "Your mom had a tough time getting up this morning," aide Kathy would sometimes say. "She was missing your Dad."

I had no idea she missed Dad. That was a real surprise to me. I guess it was her long-term memory that kept his presence alive. And, too, I had put photos of the family in a shadow box on the wall outside of her room. The largest one was of her and dad.

Once in a while, resident Mary would hand me one of her magazines. "Do you think your mom would like to look at one of my magazines? I sometimes see her reading in the lobby," she said.

I was grateful when the nursing director called if anything out of the ordinary happened to Mom ... a fall, stomach pains, vomiting. I knew they were protecting themselves; nevertheless, I appreciated it.

After Mom's three tumbles, the nursing staff stopped me more than once to say, "I'm worried about your Mom. She's not the same since she fell." Hugs and tears were plentiful during those times.

CHAPTER 42

THE DISAPPOINTMENTS

E VEN THOUGH THE perks were heartwarming, there were also disappointments. I am savvy enough to know that this is not a perfect world we live in. Yet I continuously find it discouraging when things fall through the cracks.

Most of the disappointments had to do with lack of communication. The first time I noticed it was when one of the aides disappeared from the premises of Colony.

When I asked about her whereabouts, I was told, "Oh, she's gone. Took a job in Florida." No forewarning—just poof, gone!

Staff turnover meant new faces and new names for the residents and family members to remember. It meant more effort on my part while I was grappling with this new and sudden enemy, dementia, which was breathing down my neck.

I wanted consistency. But, as my son would say, "In the ideal world Mom…." In other words, forget it.

Another example was Director Dee. More than once I told her how grateful I was to know her and work with her. She was fun and funny. Her people skills were unparalleled, her concern for the residents and families, remarkable. She spent time teasing and talking to each resident in the hallways, the lobby, or in individual rooms. I loved her.

"You can't *ever* leave here while my Mom is a resident. Got that?" I would tease, shaking my finger at her.

"I'm not going anywhere," she would say cheerfully.

Within the year she was gone. I learned of it through an announcement she made at a "family night" event. She tapped her spoon on the side of her glass to get our attention, then said, "This is my last day here. I have no other plans right now, but I'll keep in touch. I've enjoyed working with all of you and I'll miss you." End of story.

Her absence left a hole in my heart. No doubt I was selfish about wanting Dee to stay, but Mom, with her short-term memory loss, didn't even notice she was gone.

I've already mentioned about Mom's missing clothes at Selby, which now seems trivial considering the fine care she received. Still, I was surprised and disappointed when the bright yellow sign "Daughter Will Do the Laundry" was ignored.

At Creekside, Mom's last stop, my husband and I stood waiting at the extended care facility for her to arrive from the hospital. We waited … and waited … and waited.

We were told that her arrival time would be around noon, so we were there early. At 2:00 P.M., when she hadn't arrived, and no one had come to talk to us about it, I asked the receptionist to call the hospital to find out the status of Mom's transfer. She did. "Oh, they took her to a facility on the other side of town and will be here as soon as they can," she said. I was dumbfounded, but quick to recall my son's words, "In the ideal world...."

If that snafu wasn't enough, it was even worse that evening at dinnertime. A young gal, a candy striper, came into the room while I was there, smiled and placed Mom's dinner on the bedside tray.

When I removed the lid, I saw pork chops, green beans and escalloped potatoes. "Whoa, what's this?" I asked. "Her dinner," replied the girl sheepishly.

"I don't think so," I blurted, probably still mad at the earlier mix-up. I explained that Mom was no longer on solids, but on pureed foods. The girl checked the sheet of paper near the plate and told me there was nothing on the sheet that indicated pureed food.

"Take it back and find out," I fired. She picked up the tray. "This is my first day on the job," she said, adding, "Sorry."

When she returned several minutes later, pureed chili, pureed peas and pureed fruit were under the lid. I was happy to see the change, but my anger lingered. What if I had not been there? Would someone have tried to feed Mom the solids? Would Mom have choked? Died?

Again, lack of communication.

CHAPTER 43

THE PALLIATIVE CARE

IT TOOK A lot more effort to get myself over to Colony Court now that Mom and I didn't laugh together anymore. It was even hard to connect with the other residents and staff members. I never knew what would face me after I walked in.

By now the staff had to help Mom get out of bed, dressed, and into a wheelchair. The most I could do was comb her hair, brush her teeth for her, or pencil on her eyebrows. I continued to talk lovingly as I tackled each task, pretending things were the same as before.

I wondered how long it would be before Mom would not be able to stay at Colony. Colony was assisted living for folks who could exist on their own or needed a specific type of assistance, but it wasn't a long-term care facility or a nursing home. Everything seemed to be on hold.

THE PALLIATIVE CARE

I didn't have to wonder very long. Mom had one more vomiting episode where a pulse could not be found. It was the final call to 911 from Colony Court for her.

"Your mom meets the criteria for palliative care," the doctor said matter-of-factly, "so I'm sending her to that unit for recovery."

One of my pet peeves is when anyone—physicians included—talks above your head as if you aren't there, so I bellowed, "And what the deuce is palliative care?"

"Palliative care is care that deals with keeping patients as comfortable as possible … pain management, if you will. Morphine," he said.

He added, "Your mom is also eligible for hospice."

"What?" I asked, thinking that hospice was for cancer patients who had less than six months to live.

He assured me that she fit the criteria for it: weight loss, can't function on her own, dementia. He added, "Some folks are in hospice for a year or more and some actually recover." That was the good news.

The bad news was that, even though Mom's sobbing had stopped, her sleeping had increased. The only pain I observed was when an aide moved her or attempted to get her to sit on the side of the bed.

By now I had called my sister to come for support. I also called my son, niece, and nephew, all of whom lived nearby. I could not take the torment any longer by myself.

When my son walked into Mom's room, her face lit up like a Christmas tree! She leaned forward and reached for his hand. Her eyes were sparkling.

My sister and I stared at each other, our eyes sparkling, too. What a revelation! Later, we both agreed that she may have mistaken my son for her younger brother, who had been dead for forty years, but in his youth, he had looked a lot like my son.

The staff tried to get Mom up and out of bed to see how well she could walk. "We tried to get her to walk, but she couldn't manage it," they told me later. Well duh, I thought. She's been in bed for four days and was in a wheelchair most of the time before that. I probably wouldn't be able to walk either.

On Mom's fourth day there, she was discharged. We were informed that she would no longer be able to live at Colony Court. She needed round-the-clock care.

Once again, we were in a state of flux. Once again, a list of appropriate facilities was handed to me. And, once again, for practical purposes, I chose one closest to my home so I could visit regularly. New challenges would be forthcoming.

CHAPTER 44

THE GIRLS REVISITED

I FOUND CREEKSIDE Community Care to be the ideal spot for Mom's last days. Fifteen minutes from my house, fairly new, bright and cheerful. The staff was friendly.

During Mom's first week there, physical therapy was tried. She was moved from the bed onto a chair, where she sat up for an hour or two. With the help of a nurse, she could take a few steps. She was eating pureed foods on a regular basis. Mostly pudding and ice cream.

Then without warning, things changed. She was unable to eat at all.

As Karen and I entered Creekside the second week—on Girls Day—we found Mom sitting in a wheelchair across from the nursing station, in front of a blaring television set near a fish tank. The fish were darting here and there in the tank, in stark contrast to the few patients in the small lobby who sat in a comatose state. Mom was one of them, her head down on her chest, hair matted in the back.

I hated it when I saw a resident or patient with hair matted down. It was a red flag—neglect! I know it's not the job of nurses or aides to comb the hair of patients, but I wanted someone—anyone—to keep up their appearances. My problem.

My heart sank. As long as Mom was able to keep her head up, I believed she might live forever. Talk about denial!

Karen and I looked at each other with dismay, not knowing what to do or say. Karen leaned down and spoke to Mom as if nothing was different. "Hey Mom, I came to see you today. Aren't you going to talk to me? I brought some more pictures." Good ol' Karen. She wheeled Mom to her room and, with the help of an aide, was able to get her into bed.

"She sleeps most of the time," offered the aide. "That's what they do toward the end."

I shall never forget what my sister did after that. She crawled right up onto Mom's bed, put her arms around her and talked to her as if everything was all right. "You are a good mom. Do you know that?" she asked, looking down at her. The one-way conversation continued as Mom lay there with her mouth open and eyes closed.

Karen had become the parent and Mom had become the child. Karen's tenderness was one of the most loving gestures I have ever witnessed.

CHAPTER 45

THE DENIALS

BEFORE THE MOVE to Creekside, the staff at the hospital had handed me plenty of material on hospice—what it is and what it does. I placed it in the trunk of my car right beside the other information I had been given earlier on dementia.

I still hadn't read it. I used my parent's philosophy, "What I don't know won't hurt me."

My mom used to say, "If I get cancer, I don't want to know about it." She would not go to a doctor unless forced. Preventive medicine wasn't her thing. Dad was the same way. When he did go, he never asked questions, just accepted the verdict, whatever it was. Can denial be a good thing?

I finally drummed up the courage to read the pamphlets on dementia and found I had been living in denial the entire two years, sugarcoating each and every stage. But denial has a way of finally getting in your face, like a bucket of ice-cold water when it's thrown on you. Whoosh!

After I'd been going to Creekside for a week or so, a member of the cleaning staff saw me come in one day and hollered, "Your mom is in the *regular* dining room today." Since the regular dining room was where residents fed themselves, I was thrilled. I could envision her sitting at the table feeding herself and smiling.

Mom had heretofore been eating in the *small* dining room, reserved for those who needed help. I practically danced down the hall.

I entered the dining room only to find Mom sitting with her head down on her chest, brownish drool on the front of her pink sweater. "What the hell?" I wondered.

I shot a quick glance at a nearby staff member and asked, "What's going on here?"

She responded apologetically while lifting a spoonful of mashed potatoes to the mouth of another resident, "I couldn't get anything into her mouth. I tried."

Sure you did, I screamed inwardly, *What do you care? She's not "your" mom. She is one of twenty or so in this room, and you're too busy to take the time for my mom!*

I noticed that Mom's tablemates were also sitting with their heads down on their chests. I moaned quietly, "Dear God, these souls were once healthy, vibrant people—people who led active, interesting lives. Now look at them." My heart ached for *them* and my mom as they sat there like prisoners awaiting execution.

Undaunted, I knelt down and put my arm around Mom's shoulders. I thought to myself, angrily, *Well, that aide didn't try hard enough. That's the problem.*

Determined, I dipped a spoon into a bit of mashed potatoes with gravy and lifted it to her lips. "Here you go, Mom," I whispered, thinking I held some type of magical power. The potatoes and gravy slid right off the spoon onto her sweater. *Ugh!* I thought, my mind spinning like an old-fashioned top.

I slowly stood up, wiped the potatoes from Mom's sweater, and smiled. *Tomorrow will be better,* I told myself.

CHAPTER 46

THE WAILING

I GRABBED THE handles of Mom's wheelchair and whirled past the aide I had just spoken with, as if to brush off her earlier feeble attempt to feed Mom.

I hurried back past the laundry room, the beauty parlor and a fish tank, anxious to get Mom to her room to something familiar—the food channel on TV, the red geraniums lined up on the window sill like toy soldiers, the green-and-white striped afghan at the bottom of her bed—the one she had so lovingly made forty years earlier. *What do the rest of them know, anyway?* I asked myself, indignantly.

It was then and there that the bucket of water hit me, full force. They know. Of course they know. That's what they do. That's who they are—professionals.

Safely back in Mom's room, the small brownish spot of drool looming as large as a saucer, I leaned down and threw my arms around her. "Mom, oh Mom," I wailed.

"How could this be happening? I don't know what to do anymore. I visit you every day, thinking that if I do, you'll get better. But, it's not happening. I don't know what else to do."

I was finally facing reality. Two years of pent up emotions came gushing out like a tidal wave. Mom was dying. It felt like I was in a deep, black hole with no hope of getting out.

I blubbered on and on, eventually wondering if a staff member in the hall would come running into the room to see what the commotion was. No one came.

Eventually, I stood up—weak kneed—and reached over to the table tray for a handful of tissues.

After regaining my composure, I walked slowly and deliberately to the nursing station and asked, my voice cracking, "Would someone please come help me put my mom back into her bed? She needs her rest."

An unexpected feeling of calm came over me, like sand being washed away after a day at the beach. I wondered how long it would last.

CHAPTER 47

THE HOSPICE

HOSPICE WAS CALLED. A forty-ish, bright and cheerful nurse showed up to give us a heads-up on what to expect. "Lois," she said, looking at her straight on and smiling, "I'm gonna' be all over you like a second skin. Sure hope you'll warm up to me." Mom watched intently, then smiled.

At that juncture Mom was alert on and off, but not talking. I could still show her family photos. When I asked, "Mom, is that a picture of your mom?" she would smile and nod.

I remember one day, in particular, when I decided to push her up and down the long hallways that she unexpectedly made a comment.

We had just passed two large fish tanks and a handful of residents in a small lobby near the reception area, when she blurted, "It's cold right here." She was right. The February wind had just darted in through the front door as the mailman entered the facility. I was dumbfounded.

The hospice folks were amazed at Mom's resiliency and stamina. "Your Mom's vitals and her health in general are good. She simply can't eat anymore. We don't know how long she'll last."

She was now being given water through a straw with some type of thickener added to the water. It kept chapped lips at bay.

The pastor was there daily, and the nurses were more vigilant. CDs were brought in by hospice to add a soothing effect. Bibles were tucked into their bags for easy access when the notion hit them to read to her. The curtains were drawn most of the time to ensure peace and quiet.

Most of all, what hospice gave me was relief and the knowledge that Mom would be surrounded by professionals who knew the lay of the land and who were creating a loving and caring atmosphere.

I'm not sure it was the hospice staff or someone else, but I remembered these words, "You can talk to folks until the very end because the hearing is the last to go."

I bought into it anyhow, and talked with her up until the last day. While painting on her eyebrows, applying the thickened water with a straw (instead of lipstick) and combing her hair. Those gestures were my only tangible connection with my one-and-only Mom, who gave birth to me at the tender age of seventeen.

I never heard her complain about the birth or the raising of any of us four kids. We seemed to be a gift to her, as she was to us.

CHAPTER 48

THE END

"IT'S JUST A matter of time now," the nurse said as I passed by the nursing station that last day. My feet felt like cinderblocks as I headed down the long hallway to whatever awaited me.

What awaited me was silence. It hung in the air like heavy rain clouds ready to burst. There was nothing to do but sit and wait for the inevitable. I felt cold, so I kept my coat on. Was the chill from the temperature of the room or was it from the dread of imminent death?

My sister and I had been with Mom the day before. We agreed it wasn't necessary for Karen to make the three-hour trek back and forth from Cincinnati again. Mom's condition would either stay the same or worsen.

I witnessed one of the nurses turn down the blankets to check Mom's legs and feet. "When the toes begin to turn bluish, it's a sign that circulation is suspect and the end is near." At least that's what I think I heard. By that time, my mind was "mush."

THE END

I listened to Mom's labored breathing, watched her eyelids twitch now and again, felt the warmth of her hands as I held them. They were much smaller than mine—and fit right inside mine, like a child's. I took off her wedding rings and dropped them into my coat pocket. She had worn them for seventy years.

I sat there recalling how much fun Mom had always been—game for most anything, never forgot a birthday, was *always* ready to help when she was asked. When my children were born, she was there in a heartbeat to do what she was happiest doing—taking care of babies, cooking, and cleaning.

I thought about the shotgun marriage to my dad at age sixteen and the births of my three siblings and me—a house full of kids, a busy life. Mom made sure we were dressed, fed, and out the door to school; then, dressed, fed, and out the door into the big wide world itself.

She crocheted afghans for each child and grandchild; took up painting in her later years. She was active in her church, committed to baking corn soufflé for the luncheons following the funerals of local folks. This week the tables would be turned. Someone else would be baking corn soufflé for *her* family.

A hospice nurse brushed quietly past me. Nary a word as she turned on some soothing music, closed the curtains, and sat down.

"Why don't you go on home now," she solemnly urged, then continued, "I'll be here with her. We'll call you when it's time."

And they did.

THE EPILOGUE

IT'S BEEN FOUR years since Mom died. I think of her almost every day—her resourcefulness, her sense of humor, her feistiness, her beauty.

I continue to visit the residents at Colony Court. I park outside room 63, hoping she'll wave at me, knowing that she won't. Even though I am overcome with sadness every time I go there, the need to revisit the facility overrides my discomfort at being there.

In the lobby, things seem the same. The new furnishings still look fresh; staff members continue to walk back and forth in the lobby; residents still sit with the same expressions: happy, forlorn, bland. As King Solomon says in Ecclesiastes 1:9, "There is no new thing under the sun."

Maybe there is no new thing under the sun, but things are starkly different. Mom is no longer there.

My mind wanders sometimes. Did Mom really live here? Was I really here? Did I eat dinner with her and her tablemates in that very dining room? Was Mom's room number really 63? I resist the urge to walk down the long hall to check and see if she is there sitting on the edge of the bed waiting for me.

A familiar face calls my name and jolts me back to reality. Then another. "We miss you," they holler in unison. I tell them I miss them, too. That's why I still visit. It feels good to see old friends who remember Mom.

By now my heart is lighter, remembering how much I loved—and still love—Colony Court. It was the perfect spot for Mom after Dad died.

"Are you happy here, Mom?" I once asked while sitting in the lobby with her. She hesitated, then looked at me and said, "I wouldn't say happy, but 'content.'" "Content" was good enough for me.

I often wonder if I could have done more for Mom. Been more sensitive? More loving, like my sister? More patient?

In retrospect, I feel guilty that I hadn't kept our brother Dan more involved those last two months of Mom's life. He was the most emotional sibling in the family, and I remembered his words, "I can't stand to see Mom this way." So, I went with that. I believe that decision on my part may have been a mistake.

My husband refuses to let me "go there" whenever I bring up the subject of guilt. "You did a lot for your mom," he would say. "More than the average person would have done. Let it go."

He's right, of course. Instead of focusing on what I didn't do, I need to focus on what I did … how I felt.

THE EPILOGUE

I did what I thought was right at the time and, for the most part, it felt good … and right.

Mom and I had become more than mother and daughter during our two years together at Colony, Selby, and Creekside. We became friends. Pals. What more could a daughter ask?

CPSIA information can be obtained at www.ICGtesting.com
Printed in the USA
LVOW131130240113

316973LV00039B/670/P

9 781599 770499